The First-Timer's Guide to Science Experiments

The First-Timer's Guide to Science Experiments

By Natalie Goldstein
Illustrated by Janise Gates

LOWELL HOUSE JUVENILE

LOS ANGELES

NTC/Contemporary Publishing Group

Published by Lowell House
A division of NTC/Contemporary Publishing Group, Inc.
4255 West Touhy Avenue, Lincolnwood (Chicago), Illinois 60646-1975 U.S.A.

Requests for such permissions should be addressed to:
NTC/Contemporary Publishing Group, Inc.
4255 West Touhy Avenue, Lincolnwood (Chicago), Illinois 60646-1975 U.S.A.

Managing Director and Publisher: Jack Artenstein
Director of Publishing Services: Rena Copperman
Editorial Director, Juvenile: Brenda Pope-Ostrow
Director of Juvenile Development: Amy Downing
Designer: Treesha Runnells Vaux

Library of Congress Catalog Card Number: 98-75618
ISBN 0-7373-0069-8

Lowell House books can be purchased at special discounts when ordered in bulk for premiums and special sales.
Contact Customer Service at the above address, or call 1-800-323-4900.

Printed and bound in the United States of America
10 9 8 7 6 5 4 3 2 1

Contents

To Parents and Teachers

Children are naturally curious about the world and love to explore it. This book provides children with fascinating and rewarding experiments they can do themselves. Each activity begins with a question you may have heard your child ask, for example, "Where does the wind come from?" Next is a simple description that gives some background about the experiment. The description and question at the beginning of each activity will motivate your child to complete the experiment. An explanation of what happened in the experiment immediately follows.

The activities in this book are fun and safe to do. Instructions are kept as simple as possible. Performing these experiments will give a child a sense of accomplishment and an appreciation of how science works. Some activities require the assistance of an adult, for example, those using heat or a flame. You may help your child learn new vocabulary, too. All "Key Words" from the activities are defined in the Glossary at the back of the book. Join your child as he or she discovers excitement and success through science.

Key words to help give direction   Clear question to focus child   Area of science being studied

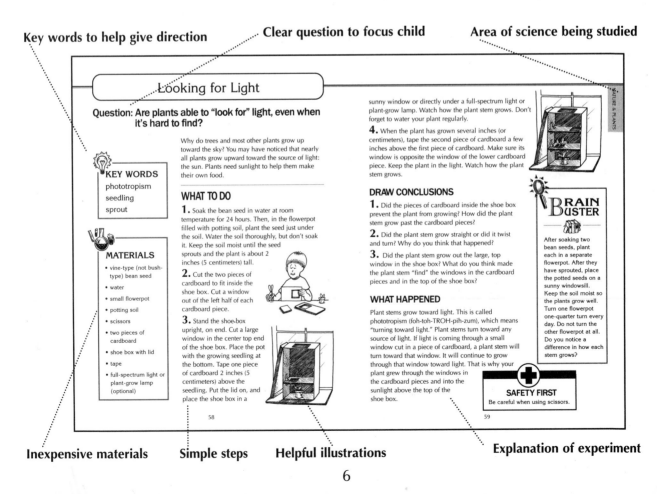

Inexpensive materials   Simple steps   Helpful illustrations   Explanation of experiment

All the materials used in these experiments are safe, inexpensive, and easy to find. Most are common household objects or substances. Here are some types of stores where you may find the materials you'll need:

Supermarket
food coloring, scissors, straws, glass jars and glasses, measuring cups and spoons, baking soda, vinegar, soda bottles, waxed paper, plastic bags, food items, wooden spoon, birdseed, paper towels, dishwashing liquid, cornstarch, lightbulbs, balloons, notebook, food scale, crayon

Drugstore
eyedropper, iodine, rubbing alcohol

Hardware Store
thumbtacks, ruler, compass, scissors, glue, window screening, cardboard, tape, string, flashlight, grease pencil, magnets, magnifying glass (hand-held lens), rubber bands, watch, cardboard tubes

Arts and Crafts Store
clay, colored paper or poster board, small mirror, balloons, yardstick, colored plastic sheets, rubber bands

Flower Shop or Garden Center
flowerpots, potting soil, sand, flowers, plants, plant sprayer

Photo Shop
photographic paper

If additional equipment is wanted, try contacting a scientific supply company, such as Edmund Scientific at 101 East Gloucester Pike, Barrington, NJ 08007 (609) 573-6250. Their catalog is extensive and prices are reasonable.

Let's Experiment!

One day many years ago, Isaac Newton was sitting under an apple tree. Newton was a very curious fellow. He was always asking questions about the world and how it worked. He wanted to know about everything. One thing he had wondered about was why people and animals stay fixed to the earth and don't go flying off into space. While Newton was dozing under the tree, it is said, an apple fell off a branch and hit him on the head. Newton had two thoughts. The first was "Ouch!" The second was "Whatever force made that apple fall off the tree is what keeps people from flying off into space!" So Newton decided to find out what that force was.

Newton went off—rubbing the bump on his head, no doubt—and began doing experiments to discover what made the apple fall to the ground. After lots of experimenting and thinking, Newton discovered and explained what we today know as the force of gravity.

You probably ask a lot of questions about how the world works, just as Isaac Newton did. Isaac Newton was one of the world's greatest scientists. Like all scientists, he asked a lot of questions. All science begins with a question: Why is the sky blue? What is the wind? How does something work? One of the best ways to answer questions like these is to do an experiment and see what happens.

BEING A SCIENTIST

Being a scientist means thinking of ways to answer interesting questions. Science is really just a matter of common sense, logical thinking, and careful observation. To be a scientist, you must

➤ **LOOK.** Notice things you would like to know about. Looking carefully at things gives you ideas about them and raises questions about how they work.

➤ **QUESTION.** When you look closely at things around you, you may have questions about them. Scientists ask lots of questions. They don't know all the answers, but they plan on finding out.

➤ **TEST.** An experiment is simply a test. Scientists design tests that will give them answers to their questions.

➤ **OBSERVE.** During an experiment, scientists look very carefully at what happens. You also need to look carefully at what happens during and at the end of an experiment. This may give you clues that help you answer your question.

➤ **RECORD.** Write down what you see. Write down what happens during and at the end of an experiment. Writing everything down helps scientists understand the results of the experiment.

> EXPERIMENT: when I shined the flashlight on.
>
> MY CONCLUSIONS:
>
> MORE QUESTIONS:

➤ **THINK.** Think about the results of your experiment. What do the results tell you? Do they answer your question? Very often, the results of an experiment raise more interesting questions.

➤ **CONCLUDE.** Decide what the test results are "telling" you, and draw conclusions. What have you learned from your experiment?

Remember, "doing science" is asking questions about things you don't know. Sometimes an experiment answers your question. Other times an experiment does not answer your question but instead makes you think of more questions! Experiments don't always turn out exactly the way you think they will. Let the results of your experiments lead you to new ideas and new questions.

BEFORE YOU DO AN EXPERIMENT

When doing the experiments in this book, be sure to do the following things first:

1. Get a parent's or another adult's permission to do the experiment.

2. Read the list of materials. Gather everything you will need.

3. Read the instructions. Make sure you understand what you have to do and how long the experiment will take.

4. Write down what you observe.

Remember, too, that there is no such thing as failure. If an experiment does not turn out as you planned, you can always do it again. Making mistakes can be useful in science. Sometimes a mistake leads to a very interesting result—and maybe even a great scientific discovery.

SAFETY FIRST!

You should be smart and safe when doing your science experiments. Some experiments use materials that only adults should handle. Have an adult be your "lab assistant." Follow these simple rules for safe science.

1. Have a grown-up present when you do experiments.

2. Plan ahead—know what materials you'll need and have them ready. Read the experiment instructions.

3. Only an adult should use anything hot or anything on or near a flame.

4. Be careful when using sharp objects, such as scissors, or have an adult use them.

5. Never taste, eat, or swallow anything you make during a science experiment. Do not touch your eyes, lips, or mouth when working with experiment materials. Always wash your hands after doing an experiment.

6. It's smart to label all the concoctions you make when you do your experiments.

7. Keep small children and pets away from your "science lab" experiment area. Tie up or pin back long hair and loose clothing.

8. Keep your science lab clean. Start on a clean surface and then clean it thoroughly when you're done.

KEEPING RECORDS

Sometimes it's difficult to remember everything that you did and everything that happened during an experiment. For this reason, it's helpful to write down what you do and what you observe. It's a good idea to keep a science notebook handy so you can write things down. Writing things down helps you remember. It also helps you analyze the results of your experiment and answer your question. Your notes may help you link something you did during an experiment with the results you got. Your notes may lead you to ask more interesting questions about your experiment.

Writing down your observations is called keeping a record of what happens during a science experiment. Get a notebook, a pad, or some paper. For each experiment, write down what you do and what you observe. You may also write down the conclusions you draw from the results of your experiments—and any new questions the results make you think of. See the next page for an example from a science notebook.

EXAMPLE OF A SCIENCE NOTEBOOK PAGE

Date:

Description of Experiment:

What is happening during the experiment?

What happened when the experiment was over?

Why do you think you got the results you did?

More questions that you have now:

The Weight of Air

Question: Does air have weight?

Is air heavy? Do things weigh more when they're full of air than when they have little or no air? Find out.

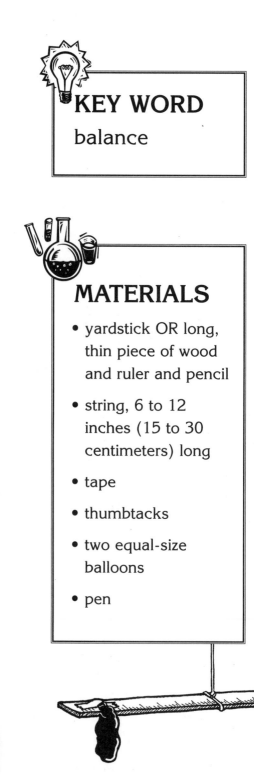

KEY WORD
balance

MATERIALS

- yardstick OR long, thin piece of wood and ruler and pencil

- string, 6 to 12 inches (15 to 30 centimeters) long

- tape

- thumbtacks

- two equal-size balloons

- pen

WHAT TO DO

1. If you are not using a yardstick, mark inches on the stick of wood, using the ruler and pencil.

2. Find the center of the yardstick or wooden stick. Tie approximately 6 to 12 inches (15 to 30 centimeters) of string around this center point and knot it. Tape the string in place if necessary. Leave enough string to dangle the stick from as you hold on to the free end of the string. Hanging there from the string, the stick should be balanced. If it is not, press thumbtacks on the side of the stick that is higher, until both sides are even. The stick is then like a balance scale.

3. Tape one empty balloon to one end of the stick. Tape the other empty balloon to the other end of the stick.

14

Make sure that you use equal lengths of tape and that the stick is still balanced. If not, move one balloon slightly until the stick is balanced and parallel to, or even with, the floor. Dangle the stick from the string to see that it is balanced.

4. With a pen, mark the places where the balloons are taped. Now that you know the empty balloons are balanced, take one balloon off the stick. Blow this balloon up until it is full of air. Tie the end of the balloon tightly so no air escapes.

5. Tape the inflated balloon back on the stick in the same spot. Dangle the stick from the string. What do you see?

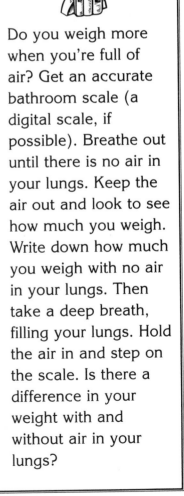

DRAW CONCLUSIONS

1. Why did the stick "scale" have to be well balanced for this experiment?

2. What happened to the stick when you attached the inflated balloon? Why do you think this happened?

WHAT HAPPENED

You saw that both balloons were balanced—were the same weight—when they had no air. When you blew up one balloon, you added air to it. The air you blew into the balloon made it get "fat." When you attached the inflated balloon to the stick, it was no longer balanced. It was weighted down by the inflated balloon because the air in that balloon made the balloon heavier.

BRAIN BUSTER

Do you weigh more when you're full of air? Get an accurate bathroom scale (a digital scale, if possible). Breathe out until there is no air in your lungs. Keep the air out and look to see how much you weigh. Write down how much you weigh with no air in your lungs. Then take a deep breath, filling your lungs. Hold the air in and step on the scale. Is there a difference in your weight with and without air in your lungs?

Balloon in a Bottle

Question: Does air take up space?

Try to blow up a balloon in a bottle and find out if an empty bottle is really empty.

....

KEY WORD

inflate

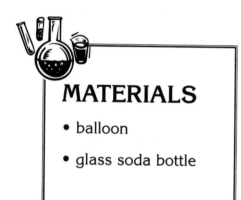

MATERIALS

- balloon
- glass soda bottle

WHAT TO DO

1. Hold on to the open end of the balloon as you push the closed part into a clean, dry soda bottle.

2. Stretch the open end of the balloon over the lip of the bottle. Make sure the balloon end fits tightly on the mouth of the bottle.

3. Try to blow up the balloon. Blow into the balloon as hard as you can. Does the balloon inflate, or expand with air?

DRAW CONCLUSIONS

1. What do you think prevented the balloon from inflating inside the bottle?

2. What was stronger, the pressure inside the bottle or the air you were blowing out of your lungs into the balloon?

WHAT HAPPENED

Though the bottle looked empty, it really was full—of air! Air takes up space. As you tried to inflate the balloon, it began to take up more space in the bottle. The balloon wouldn't inflate because of the air trapped inside the bottle. The air in the bottle was trapped there when you sealed the bottle top with the balloon. The "bottled air" pressed hard on the balloon you tried to inflate. You couldn't blow up the balloon in the bottle because the air had no space in which to expand.

trapped air presses on the balloon, allowing the balloon no room to expand

BRAIN BUSTER

Air space can keep an underwater paper towel dry. Stuff a paper towel securely into an empty juice glass. Make sure the towel doesn't fall out when you turn the glass over. Fill a large pot with cool water. Hold the glass straight upside down and plunge it into the pot of water. Wait a few seconds. Then carefully lift the glass out of the water. If you held the glass perfectly straight throughout this experiment, the paper towel in the glass will be dry. The air in the glass (between the paper towel and the glass rim) kept the water out—so the paper towel stayed dry.

Seeing Some Sound

Question: Can the effects of sound vibrations be seen?

KEY WORD

vibration

You hear sound when something causes the air to vibrate, or move rapidly. There is a way you can "see" sound vibrations that are moving through the air. Just try it!

WHAT TO DO

1. Place the plastic bowl facedown on the plastic bag. Cut the bag around the bowl, a bit larger than the outline of the bowl.

2. Turn the bowl right side up, and place the plastic over the opening. Stretch the plastic tightly and secure it with the rubber band. Tape all the edges of the plastic bag to the bowl.

3. Carefully place some rice grains or orzo pasta in the middle of the firmly stretched plastic.

MATERIALS

- heavy-duty black plastic garbage bag

- small plastic bowl (margarine container; for example)

- scissors

- rubber band (to fit around bowl)

- tape

- uncooked rice or orzo pasta

- large pot, 2–3 quart (2–3 liters) size

- wooden spoon

4. Set the large pot on its side with the opening close to the bowl, but not touching it. Hit the bottom of the pot with the wooden spoon. Watch what happens to the grains on the plastic stretched over the bowl.

DRAW CONCLUSIONS

1. What caused the grains on the plastic to jump?

2. How might the grains move differently if you hit the bottom of the pot more softly? If you hit it much harder?

WHAT HAPPENED

When you hit the bottom of the pot with the spoon, the air began to vibrate. This vibration traveled to the plastic-covered bowl. The moving air (the vibration) caused the stretched plastic to move, too. When the stretched plastic moved, the grains that were on it moved as well. The moving grains showed you that the air was moving—that sound is a vibration in air.

SAFETY FIRST
Be careful when using scissors.

BRAIN BUSTER

Make bottle music! Get several bottles of the same kind and size (soda bottles, for example). Fill one bottle with water to within 1 inch (2.5 centimeters) of the top. Leave 2 inches (5 centimeters) of air in the second bottle, 3 inches (8 centimeters) of air in the next bottle, and so on. Each bottle should have 1 inch (2.5 centimeters) less water than the previous bottle. Line the bottles up and blow across the top of ea~ make ʒ sour a ʒ

Make Light Photos

Question: How are images made on photo paper without using a camera?

When you take a photograph, the light entering the camera makes a picture on the light-sensitive film. The image on the film makes a picture when light shines through it onto special light-sensitive paper. But did you know that you can make "light photos" without a camera?

KEY WORDS

light-sensitive

silhouette

MATERIALS

- scissors

- heavy black construction paper

- black-and-white photographic paper

- assorted objects (leaf, feather, hair clip, etc.)

- ...mp

WHAT TO DO

1. Cut the black construction paper until it is about half the size of a sheet of photographic paper. Then cut any interesting shapes you like out of the black construction paper. You should first punch a hole in the paper, then cut out your shape, keeping all edges of the paper intact.

2. Darken the room as much as possible. Take out one sheet of photographic paper. Very quickly, put the black construction paper with the shapes cut

20

out of it on one-half of the photo paper and the assorted objects on the other half. Do not move anything once it's on the photo paper. Turn on the lamp so the light shines directly on the photo paper. Leave the lamp on for about 1 minute. Then turn it off.

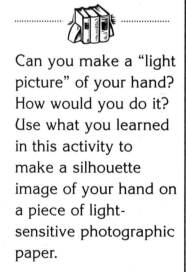

3. Take the black construction paper and the assorted objects off the photo paper. You will see that a "light picture" is left on the photo paper. (But not for long!)

DRAW CONCLUSIONS

1. In what way are the images in the "light picture" like a photograph? In what way are they different?

2. What do you think caused the "light picture" images to form on the photo paper?

3. After several minutes, the "light pictures" you made will begin to disappear. The photo paper starts to turn black. Why do you think this happens?

WHAT HAPPENED

Light-sensitive chemicals on photographic paper turn black when exposed to light. Your "light images" were made because the black construction paper and assorted objects you put on the photo paper blocked the light, preventing it from reaching the paper. The images you made were silhouettes—like shadows—of the objects that blocked the light. Several minutes after the experiment, light in the room made the light-sensitive paper turn black and the "light pictures" disappear.

BRAIN BUSTER

Can you make a "light picture" of your hand? How would you do it? Use what you learned in this activity to make a silhouette image of your hand on a piece of light-sensitive photographic paper.

SAFETY FIRST
Be careful when using scissors.

Rainbow in Your Room

Question: What colors is sunlight made of?

The sunlight that's all around you makes everything bright and easy to see. It seems to be white—or colorless. But sunlight is really made up of many different colors of light. In this experiment, you will separate sunlight into its many colors. You will make a rainbow.

KEY WORDS

prism

rainbow

refract

spectrum

wavelength

WHAT TO DO

1. Fill the shallow bowl about two-thirds full with water. Place the mirror in the bowl, resting it on the side of the bowl, so it is angled.

2. Make the room as dark as possible. Then shine the flashlight toward the mirror.

3. Look at the ceiling. What do you see?

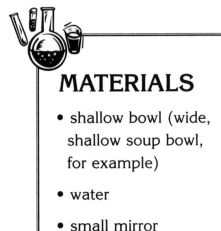

MATERIALS

• shallow bowl (wide, shallow soup bowl, for example)

• water

• small mirror

• flashlight

DRAW CONCLUSIONS

1. How do you think the water helped in producing the rainbow?

2. What colors did you see in your ceiling rainbow? In what order did they appear?

WHAT HAPPENED

A prism is anything that can separate white light, such as sunlight or light from a flashlight, into its different colors. The seven different colors that make up white light are called a spectrum. Each color has a different wavelength. For example, red has a long wavelength; blue has a short wavelength. In this case, water acted as a prism. The water refracted, or bent, the light according to each color's wavelength. Each color making up white light is bent in a slightly different way, so the colors appeared separated on the ceiling. You probably saw up to seven colors—red, orange, yellow, green, blue, indigo (a dark blue), violet (purple)—reflected on the ceiling. The colors you saw are all part of sunlight.

A rainbow is sunlight refracted through water vapor in the air. Water droplets float in the air after a rainstorm. Sunlight strikes the droplets and, if the angle is right, the light is refracted and reflected off the droplets in such a way that the light is separated into an arc of colors—a rainbow.

BRAIN BUSTER

You can buy a small prism and make your own rainbows without water. Hold the prism in the sun and make rainbows on the wall. In what order do you see the colors in the spectrum? Why do you think the colors of the spectrum are always in the same order?

All From One, One From All

Question: What colors can you make from red, yellow, and blue?

The white light you experience as sunlight really contains many colors, including red, blue, and yellow. You can mix and match these three colors, called the primary colors, to make lots of different colors. See how many colors you can make.

WHAT TO DO

1. Cut each plastic sheet into 2-inch (5-centimeter) strips. Place a yellow strip on the paper. Cover it with a blue strip. What color do you see? Cover these two strips with another yellow strip. What happens to the color?

2. Place a red strip on the white paper. Cover it with a blue strip. What color do you see? Cover these with a yellow strip or another red strip. What happens to the color?

MATERIALS

- three transparent plastic sheets: one each of red, yellow, and blue

- scissors

- sheet of white paper

3. Use the color strips, one over the other, to make as many colors as possible. How many colors did you make? Which ones?

DRAW CONCLUSIONS

1. What two colored strips make the color green? What strips together make the color orange?

2. What did you do to make a color lighter or darker? For example, how would you turn a dark green into a light green?

3. Why might there be no limit to the number of colors you can make out of red, blue, and yellow?

WHAT HAPPENED

All colors we can see are made from combinations of many colors, including red, blue, and yellow. By adding or taking away different color strips, you saw how colors combine to make many different colors.

BRAIN BUSTER

You know you can make colors out of red, blue, and yellow. But did you know that white is a color that contains all other colors? Cut a circle out of cardboard or heavy art paper. Have an adult make a hole exactly in the center of the circle. Color exactly one-third of the circle red, one-third of the circle blue, and one-third of the circle yellow. Make a top by pushing a pencil, point down, through the hole in the circle's center. Be sure that the colored side of the circle is on top. Spin your top quickly and watch what happens to the colors. If your top spins fast enough, all the colors will blend together and become white.

✚ SAFETY FIRST

Be careful when using scissors.

Thar' She Blows!

Question: What chemical reaction causes a home-made volcano to erupt?

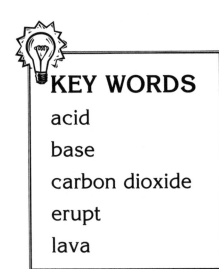

KEY WORDS

acid

base

carbon dioxide

erupt

lava

MATERIALS

- sand or potting soil

- large flat metal tray (like a cookie sheet with sides)

- small container with one end removed (soup can, for example)

- baking soda

- measuring cup with pitcher or spout

- red food coloring

- white vinegar

Have a volcano explode in your own home! Use chemistry and build your own volcano that erupts with red flowing lava. Your erupting volcano will look like the real thing—but it's not dangerous.

WHAT TO DO

1. Form the sand or soil into a mound on the flat tray. Set the small container, closed side down, on top of the soil.

2. Put ½ cup (118 milliliters) baking soda in the small container through the open top, and press the container into the top of your "mountain." Then pile the sand or soil up around the container until it is hidden (but don't cover the open top).

3. In the pitcher, add enough red food coloring to ½ cup (118 milliliters) vinegar to make it look like lava, the superhot material that oozes out of real volcanoes.

4. Quickly pour the red vinegar into the container in the top of your "mountain." Then stand back and watch what happens.

DRAW CONCLUSIONS

1. Did you hear a hissing or bubbling sound as the vinegar hit the baking soda? Did you see any bubbles? What do you think caused the sound and the bubbles?

2. What two substances do you think were involved in this chemical reaction?

WHAT HAPPENED

Baking soda is a substance called a base. Vinegar is a substance called an acid. When this acid and this base come into contact, a chemical reaction occurs. In this experiment, carbon dioxide gas is produced (that's where the hissing and bubbles came from). The gas bubbles forced the red vinegar out of the container and down the sides of your "volcano." The volcano erupted, or exploded.

DID YOU KNOW?

Inside a real volcano is a long tube, or chamber, that extends deep down into the earth. The inside of the earth is so hot, rocks and metals melt and flow there like liquids. Many hot gases are also inside a volcano. When the pressure of the hot gases gets too high, the volcano erupts. The gases under pressure force the melted rock out of the volcano. The melted rock, called lava, may shoot out the top of the volcano or may ooze down the sides of the mountain. Burning hot gases may explode hundreds of feet into the air.

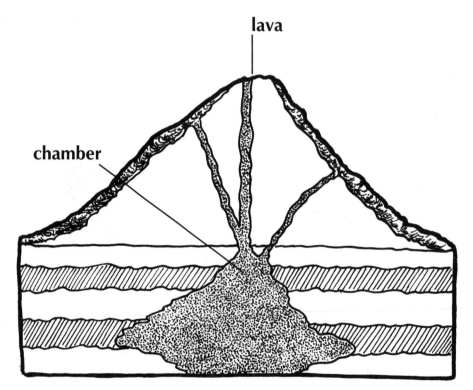

lava

chamber

Leaky Limestones

Question: Are some rocks in my neighborhood made out of limestone?

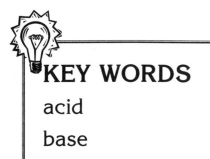

KEY WORDS

acid

base

calcium

chemical reaction

compound

limestone

vinegar

MATERIALS

- tool for digging
- paper bag
- running water
- liquid soap
- plates (one for each rock dug up)
- white vinegar
- tablespoon

You have probably seen lots of rocks in your backyard or in the park. Have you ever wondered what the rocks are made of? Some rocks may be made of a kind of stone called limestone. In this experiment, you will test rocks to see if they contain limestone.

WHAT TO DO

1. Take the digging tool and the paper bag to the park or your backyard. Collect as many different kinds of rocks as you can. If necessary, use the tool to dig up some small rocks. Place the rocks in the paper bag to carry them home.

2. Carefully wash each rock under running water, using the liquid soap. Rinse them thoroughly and let them dry.

3. Place one rock on each plate. Spoon 1 tablespoon (15 milliliters) vinegar over the rock. Watch what happens. Write down in your science notebook what you see. Did you see any bubbly "fizz" on the rock?

4. Repeat step 3 for all the rocks you collected. Did any of the rocks bubble and fizz?

5. Place together all the rocks that bubbled and fizzed.

DRAW CONCLUSIONS

1. Did any of the rocks you tested have limestone in them? How do you know?

2. Were there more rocks with limestone or without limestone in your rock collection?

3. Do you think there are lots of limestone rocks or few limestone rocks in your area? Explain your answer.

4. Do the rocks that contain limestone look similar in some way? What might you look for in other rocks that would tell you if they contain limestone?

WHAT HAPPENED

Limestone contains a calcium compound that is a base. The calcium in limestone comes from the shells of shellfish that died millions of years ago. Vinegar is a substance that is a mild acid. The scientific name for vinegar is *acetic* [uh-SEE-tik] *acid*. When an acid is added to a base, a chemical reaction takes place. In this case, acid in the vinegar reacted with the calcium base in the limestone to form bubbles, or "fizz."

SAFETY FIRST

Don't touch your eyes if your fingers are wet with vinegar. Wash your hands first.

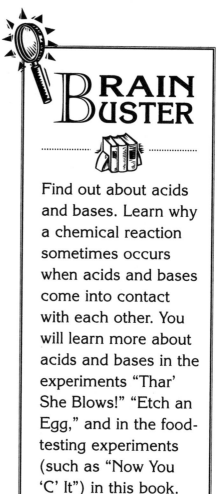

BRAIN BUSTER

Find out about acids and bases. Learn why a chemical reaction sometimes occurs when acids and bases come into contact with each other. You will learn more about acids and bases in the experiments "Thar' She Blows!" "Etch an Egg," and in the food-testing experiments (such as "Now You 'C' It") in this book.

Etch an Egg

Question: How can an eggshell be etched?

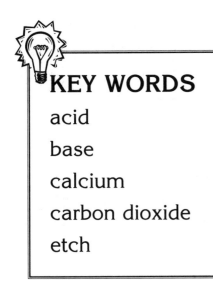

KEY WORDS

acid

base

calcium

carbon dioxide

etch

MATERIALS

- egg
- small pan
- water
- crayon or grease pencil
- clear glass jar (big enough to fit an egg)
- white vinegar

You can "print" your name or make a design on an egg. And you won't break the egg either. The secret is using chemistry.

WHAT TO DO

1. Have an adult hard-boil an egg in the small pan of water. Allow the egg to cool to room temperature.

2. Use a crayon or a grease pencil to write your name or draw a simple picture or design on the egg's shell.

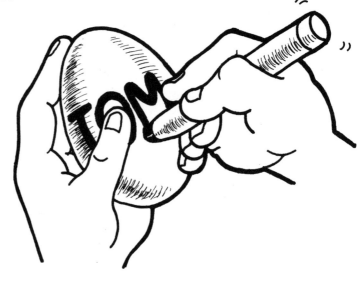

3. Fill the jar about three-fourths full with vinegar. Place the egg gently in the jar. The vinegar should cover the egg.

4. Every few hours, gently touch the egg to see if the crayon marks feel slightly raised above the rest of the eggshell. When you feel the raised crayon marks, remove the egg from the jar and rinse the egg. Carefully wipe off the crayon marks. You will see that the eggshell is etched, or eaten away, everywhere except around the raised markings.

DRAW CONCLUSIONS

1. Why do you think you had to use a waxy crayon or grease pencil for your design or name?

2. Did you see bubbles in the jar while the egg was in the vinegar? What do you think they were?

3. What do you think the vinegar does to the substance the eggshell is made of?

WHAT HAPPENED

An eggshell is made out of calcium, a mineral also found in milk. Eggshell material is called a base. A base is a substance that reacts chemically with any substance that is an acid. In this experiment, vinegar was the acid. The chemical reaction between the eggshell and the vinegar produced a gas: carbon dioxide. This gas was produced as vinegar "ate away" at the eggshell during the chemical reaction. The waxy crayon or grease pencil markings protected the marked parts of the shell from the effects of the 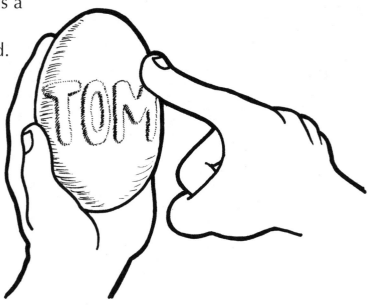 vinegar. So these marked parts of the shell were not eaten away. That's why you felt them raised above the rest of the shell.

DID YOU KNOW?

Many public statues are made out of a stone called limestone, which contains a substance that is a base. What happens when acid rain, a kind of air pollution that comes from factory smokestacks, falls on the statues? The acid in the rain eats away at the statues—because the stone they are made from is a base. In many cities, such as Rome, in Italy, beautiful old statues and sculptures are being destroyed as the acid in rain reacts with limestone. (See the "Leaky Limestones" activity on page 29.)

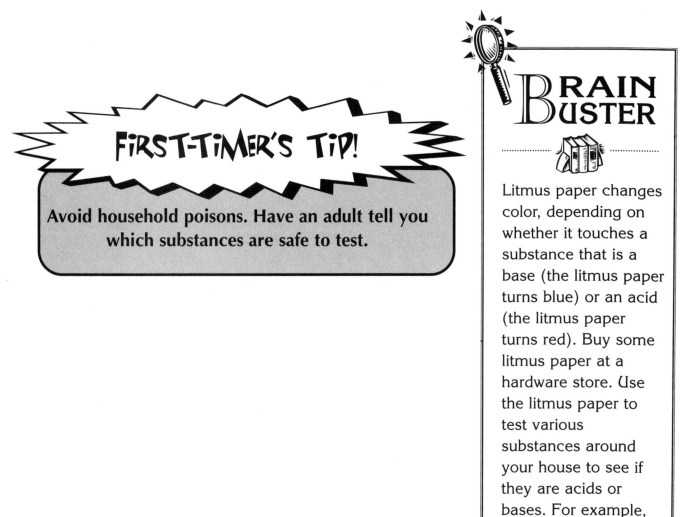

FIRST-TIMER'S TIP!

Avoid household poisons. Have an adult tell you which substances are safe to test.

BRAIN BUSTER

Litmus paper changes color, depending on whether it touches a substance that is a base (the litmus paper turns blue) or an acid (the litmus paper turns red). Buy some litmus paper at a hardware store. Use the litmus paper to test various substances around your house to see if they are acids or bases. For example, test orange juice, milk, detergent, and other safe substances.

Now You "C" It

Question: How can food be tested to see if it contains vitamin C?

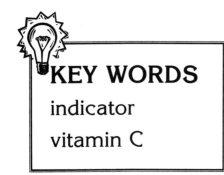

KEY WORDS

indicator

vitamin C

MATERIALS

- water
- small pan
- spoon
- cornstarch
- iodine
- eyedropper
- various juices (orange, tomato, apple, grape, etc.)
- clear juice glasses (one for each juice)

You need vitamin C to stay healthy. But how do you know what foods contain vitamin C? This activity will show you how to test foods to learn which contain the most vitamin C.

WHAT TO DO

1. Have an adult boil 1 cup (237 milliliters) water in a small pan. Then stir 1 teaspoon (5 milliliters) cornstarch into it. Allow to cool.

2. Draw up some iodine into the eyedropper. Slowly add drops of iodine, one at a time, to the water until it is blue. The blue water is your indicator, a substance that will show you, or indicate, how much vitamin C different kinds of juices have. Once your indicator is made, rinse the eyedropper with running water.

3. Pour about 1 inch (2.5 centimeters) of one of the juices into a clear, clean juice glass.

4. Draw up some indicator into the clean eyedropper. Start dropping the indicator, one drop at a time, into the juice. Count the number of drops needed to make the blue indicator color disappear into the juice. Record the number of drops in your science notebook.

5. Repeat steps 3 and 4 with each juice you wish to test. Use fresh indicator for each juice tested.

DRAW CONCLUSIONS

1. Which juice contained the most vitamin C? How many drops of indicator did you use for this juice?

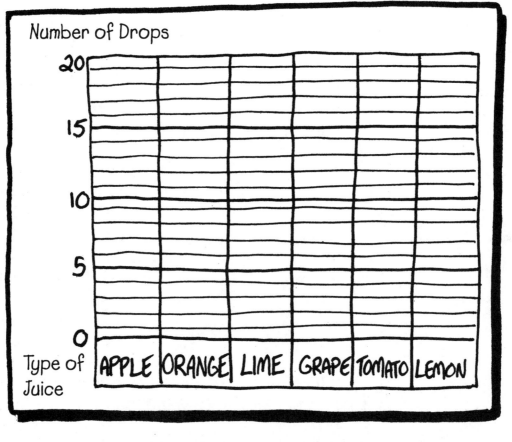

Number of Drops

20
15
10
5
0

Type of Juice

APPLE ORANGE LIME GRAPE TOMATO LEMON

✚ SAFETY FIRST

Have an adult boil the water for you.

Do not swallow iodine or put it in your mouth.

Do not drink the indicator or the juices you tested with indicator.

2. Which juice contained the least vitamin C? How many drops of indicator did you use for this juice?

3. Why did you need to use fresh indicator for each juice tested?

4. Make a graph of your test results, based on the results you recorded.

WHAT HAPPENED

The indicator reacted chemically with vitamin C. The more vitamin C a juice had, the more quickly the chemical reaction occurred. That is why juices needing many drops of indicator had less vitamin C than juices needing only a few drops of indicator.

BRAIN BUSTER

What effect does heat have on the vitamin C in juice? Use fresh indicator to test for vitamin C. After you do the steps on pages 35 and 36, have an adult put one of the juices in a pot and boil it. With an adult's help, remove the pot from the stove and let it cool for 1 minute. Then test the boiled juice with indicator. How many drops did you need before the blue disappeared? Does heat increase or destroy the vitamin C in juices?

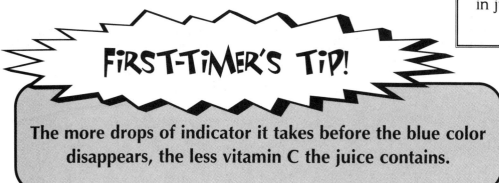

FiRST-TiMER'S TiP!

The more drops of indicator it takes before the blue color disappears, the less vitamin C the juice contains.

Sweet Scents—Make Your Own Perfume

Question: How is perfume made?

What is your favorite perfume scent? Is it rose or jasmine or vanilla? Perfume can be made from many different kinds of plants. In this activity, you will learn how perfume is made by creating your own.

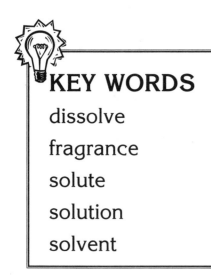

KEY WORDS

dissolve

fragrance

solute

solution

solvent

MATERIALS

- plant part for scent (clove, vanilla bean, rose petals, lavender, lilac, etc.)

- black plastic film canister

- rubbing alcohol

- tablespoon

WHAT TO DO

1. Place about 2 tablespoons (30 milliliters) rose petals (or 1 clove or ½ vanilla bean), or the equivalent amount of the "scent" plant you are using, into the film canister. (Note: If you don't have a film canister, use the smallest clean covered container you can find. Paint the outside of the container black or cover it with heavy black plastic, like a heavy-duty garbage bag, to prevent light from affecting the perfume.)

2. Add about 2 tablespoons (30 milliliters) rubbing alcohol to the canister, enough to cover the "scent" plant.

3. Cover the canister tightly. Shake it. Leave it in a cool, dark place.

4. Shake the canister briskly once a day for seven days (do not open it!). After one week, test the perfume you made by opening the container and dabbing a bit of the solution on your wrist. Take a whiff. You smell great!

DRAW CONCLUSIONS

1. Where did the scent of your perfume come from?

2. What do you think the function of the rubbing alcohol was?

WHAT HAPPENED

Perfume is a solution, a mixture in which one substance disappears into another. For example, salt water is a solution in which salt dissolves, or mixes into, water. Science calls salt the solute and water the solvent. When making the perfume, the sweet-smelling plant part was the solute and the rubbing alcohol the solvent. The rubbing alcohol drew the sweet-smelling chemicals out of the plant part. These fragrant chemicals mixed with the alcohol to form a perfume solution.

DID YOU KNOW?

It takes 1,100 pounds (500 kilograms) of rose petals to make less than 1 ounce (about 500 grams) of rose essence for perfume. No wonder perfume is so expensive!

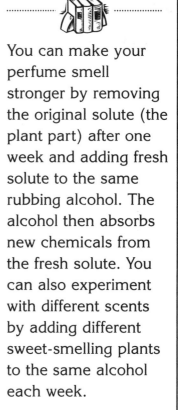

BRAIN BUSTER

You can make your perfume smell stronger by removing the original solute (the plant part) after one week and adding fresh solute to the same rubbing alcohol. The alcohol then absorbs new chemicals from the fresh solute. You can also experiment with different scents by adding different sweet-smelling plants to the same alcohol each week.

Here and Gone

Question: What makes invisible ink appear?

Write secret messages with invisible ink! Find out how something that is in the air you breathe can make invisible writing appear like magic.

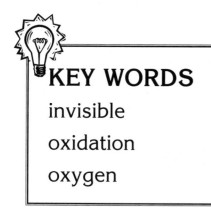

KEY WORDS

invisible

oxidation

oxygen

MATERIALS

- juice glass or small glass bowl

- sugar

- water

- matchstick or cotton-tip swab

- white writing paper

- lamp with incandescent lightbulb

WHAT TO DO

1. In the glass or bowl, mix 1 tablespoon (15 milliliters) sugar in about 2 inches (5 centimeters) of water. Stir well until the sugar is dissolved. The sugar water is your ink.

2. Dip the wooden end of the matchstick or tip of the cotton swab in the sugar water, and write your name or a message with this ink on the white paper. Let the ink dry completely. Your message will be invisible.

3. Set up a lamp with no lamp shade. Turn it on.

4. Have an adult hold up the paper near the heat of the lightbulb. In a little while, you will see your name or your message appear on the paper.

DRAW CONCLUSIONS

1. Why was your sugar and water "ink" invisible?

2. Why do you think the heat of the lightbulb made your message appear on the paper?

WHAT HAPPENED

The sugar and water solution was invisible—it couldn't be seen—because the sugar disappeared when it dissolved in the colorless water. But when the sugar was heated by the lightbulb, some chemicals in the sugar combined with the oxygen in the air. This chemical reaction, called oxidation, caused those chemicals in the sugar to turn brown. When heat made the sugar on your paper turn brown, you could then read your secret message.

SAFETY FIRST

Do not drink your invisible ink solution.

Be careful around the heat of the lightbulb.

BRAIN BUSTER

You can make invisible ink with other liquids. Try writing your secret message using lemon juice, milk, or vinegar. (You don't have to mix these with water.) Have an adult hold your messages up to the heat of a lightbulb and see what happens. Heat causes oxidation of many substances.

Stringing Water Along—Shocking Shoelaces

Question: How do we know that water molecules move?

Water is always on the move. Tiny bits of water, called molecules (MAH-luh-kyoolz), are forever bumping around and into each other. Molecules also love to travel. Find out how.

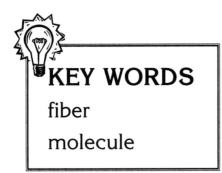

KEY WORDS

fiber

molecule

MATERIALS

- measuring cup
- water
- four small bowls or cups
- food coloring (four colors)
- long piece of white string (preferably cotton) or a long white shoelace

WHAT TO DO

1. Put about ½ cup (118 milliliters) water into each bowl or cup. Add a different color of food coloring to each bowl of water. (The more food coloring you add, the deeper the color will be.)

2. Wet the string or shoelace with water and "snake" it from one bowl to the other. Do not push it deep into the water. Only one "bend" in the string should be below the surface of the water in each bowl. There should be white string visible between the bowls.

3. Watch what happens to the string or shoelace. Is it picking up color? Leave it for a while, checking on it until it has absorbed all the color it can. Then remove the string or shoelace and let it dry. (If you want, repeat these steps to make a matching, colorful shoelace.)

DRAW CONCLUSIONS

1. Did the whole string or shoelace absorb color?

2. Bits of water stick to one another (that's why water forms "drops") and help one another move. Why, then, do you think this experiment works best if the string or shoelace is wet, not dry?

WHAT HAPPENED

String is a fiber, a material that contains many threads with lots of tiny tubelike spaces in between. Water molecules can move up these tubelike spaces and are then absorbed by the fiber. These molecules (small units of matter) stick to one another—as some water molecules move up into the fiber, the water molecules below stick to them. So the lower molecules are also dragged up into the fiber and absorbed. That's how the water molecules moved through the string or shoelace. Water molecules are so strong, they continually drag more and more water molecules up behind them.

BRAIN BUSTER

Watch water molecules on the move. Fill a clear glass jar three-fourths full with water. Add a few drops of food coloring. DO NOT STIR! What do you see? Notice the way the food coloring first sinks to the bottom, leaving a trail of color behind it. The food coloring drops are breaking up because they are being hit constantly by water molecules. If you keep watching the jar, you will see the food coloring spread evenly throughout the water. The water molecules bounce the food coloring around until it mixes thoroughly all through the water in the jar.

Multicolored Carnations

Question: How does water move through a plant?

All plants need water. But how does a tall tree get water to its top leaves? Plants have a special way of moving water from their roots, through their stems, to all their parts.

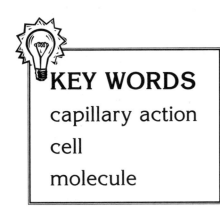

KEY WORDS
capillary action
cell
molecule

MATERIALS

- two glasses
- water
- food coloring (two colors)
- white carnation
- ruler
- knife or scissors

WHAT TO DO

1. Fill the glasses about three-fourths full with water. Add one food coloring to one glass of water, and the other food coloring to the other glass. Add enough food coloring to get a good, strong color. Place the glasses next to each other in a warm room.

2. Have an adult cut the stem of the carnation to about 8 inches (20 centimeters) long. Remove any leaves from the stem. Then have the adult carefully cut the lower 5 inches (13 centimeters) of the stem in half lengthwise. Be careful the stem is not crushed.

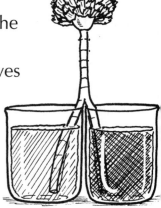

3. Gently place one split stem in one glass of colored water, and put the other split stem in the other glass of different-colored water. Adjust the glasses to make sure the split stems stay in the water and the flower stands upright between

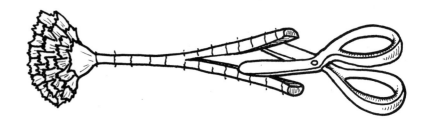

the two glasses. Let the flower absorb the water for several hours, until you see the petals changing color. Check on the flower every hour to see how it changes.

DRAW CONCLUSIONS

1. Did the carnation's petals change color? What colors did the petals become?

2. What part of the plant "drank up" the colored water and carried it to the flower?

3. If you had split the stem into three parts and put each part in a glass with different food coloring, how many colors do you think the flower would then have?

WHAT HAPPENED

Water moves through a plant's stem by a process called capillary (CAP-ih-leh-ree) action. In this experiment, you saw that the colored water traveled all the way to the flower petals. Inside the plant stem are long, thin tubes made of tiny structures called cells. Tiny units of water, called molecules, "climb" the narrow stem cells. Water molecules tend to stick to each other (that's why water forms drops). As water molecules climb into the stem cells, more water molecules follow. The water molecules are so tightly packed in the stem cells, they become strong enough to pull more water molecules up behind them. In this way, the water molecules move up through the cells and draw more water after them. The water moves up and up until the whole plant has had enough to drink.

BRAIN BUSTER

Does temperature affect capillary action? Cut about 1 to 2 inches (2.5 to 5 centimeters) off the bottom of two stalks of celery. Mix glasses of water with food coloring, and place one stalk of celery in each glass. Place one glass in a warm room. Place the other glass in the refrigerator. Observe both for several hours. What can you conclude about the effect of temperature on the capillary action that draws water up a celery stalk?

SAFETY FIRST

Be careful when using scissors.

Water Ball Race

Question: Why does water "race" over certain surfaces?

Forget your favorite game—it's time to have a water ball race. Make your own water drop racer and see if you can win.

KEY WORDS

adhere

cohere

MATERIALS

- waxed paper
- ruler
- grease pencil
- measuring cup
- water
- three cups
- food coloring (three colors)
- eyedropper
- three straws

WHAT TO DO

1. Prepare the "race course" on a piece of waxed paper, 12 inches (31 centimeters) long. Use the ruler and grease pencil to mark off the "starting line" and the "finish line" on opposite sides of the paper. Then connect these two lines with three "tracks" (each about 3 inches, or 8 centimeters, wide), which each water drop will race on. (This experiment is based on three water racers, but you can adjust it to have fewer or more.)

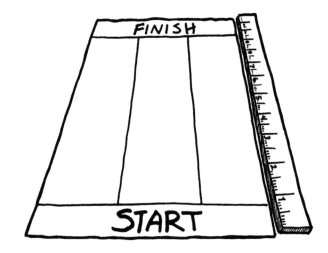

2. Put ½ cup (118 milliliters) water into each of three cups. Mix a different color of food coloring into each cup. Draw water into the eyedropper, and then release a few drops onto the waxed paper at the starting line on one of the tracks of the race course. This will make your "racing drop." Repeat this for the other racers. Each racer has a different color drop, but all water drops should be the same size.

3. At the word *go*, each racer puts the straw to his or her lips and begins blowing a water drop across the race course toward the finish line. Do not blow too hard, or the water drop may break up. Make sure the drop stays in its track. If the drop breaks up or leaves the track, make a new drop and begin again at the starting line. The water drop that crosses the finish line first wins.

DRAW CONCLUSIONS

1. Why do you think it was important to use waxed paper for your race course?

2. What do you think would have happened if you had used a paper towel? (Try it—drop water on a paper towel and see what happens.)

3. Why do you think the water drop stayed together as you blew on it and it moved along the track?

WHAT HAPPENED

Water adheres to, or stays on, many surfaces. In science, the word *adhere* means "to stick to a substance that is different." For example, water adheres to the slippery surface of waxed paper. But water coheres to itself. *Cohere* means "to stick to something that is the same." Water molecules stick to—or cohere to—other water molecules. That's why your racing ball (drop) of water stayed together. Sometimes, though, if a force is powerful enough, it can separate water molecules. If you blew on your water drop too hard, the force of your breath may have separated the molecules of water. If you blew with just the right amount of force, the water drop stuck to itself and to the surface of the waxed paper as you moved it toward the finish line.

A paper towel is a fiber that has many tubelike threads, as do some cloth fabrics. These tubes absorb the water, so the water does not remain as a drop on top of the fiber.

BRAIN BUSTER

Stretch water with air. Mix together in a container: 2 cups (500 milliliters) water, 1 tablespoon (15 milliliters) sugar, and ¼ cup (59 milliliters) dishwashing liquid. Put the cap on the container and shake well. After the liquid settles and the foam is gone, pour it into a bowl. Bend the end of a hanger into a ring. Dip the ring into the liquid, and then blow on one side of it. You're blowing bubbles! Your breath pushes on the water molecules that are sticking together (cohering), and expands them to make a colorful bubble. If they expand too much (if you blow too hard), the molecules separate and your bubble bursts!

Grapes Lose Weight

Question: What happens to grapes when they "lose weight"?

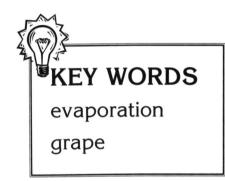

KEY WORDS

evaporation

grape

MATERIALS

- scissors
- cardboard
- grapes
- tape
- two plastic window screens
- food scale
- two long strings

Sometimes people go on a diet to lose weight. People may also make certain kinds of fruits "lose weight." Do you know what grapes that lose weight are called? By the end of this experiment, you will!

WHAT TO DO

1. Have an adult help you cut a hole out of the center of the cardboard. The hole should be large enough to enclose ⅛ pound (2 ounces, or .07 grams) grapes.

2. If necessary, have an adult cut the screens to fit over the cardboard hole. Use tape to attach one plastic screen over the hole.

3. Copy the chart below in your science notebook.

WEIGHT OF GRAPES BEFORE DRYING	WEIGHT OF GRAPES AFTER DRYING

4. Put the grapes on the food scale. Write in the chart how much the grapes weigh.

5. One by one, place the grapes on the screen taped to the cardboard. Then cover the grapes with the second screen. Tape this screen in place over the grapes to secure them.

6. Tape the strings to the bottom of the cardboard, so the cardboard can hang evenly from them. Hang the cardboard outside, above the ground, in a place that is sunny during the day.

7. Leave the cardboard outside during the day, for about 7 days, until the grapes look dried up. (Don't leave the cardboard out at night or on rainy days.)

8. When the grapes look wrinkled and dry, bring them inside and remove them from the screened cardboard. Weigh the wrinkled grapes, or raisins, on the food scale. Record the weight in your chart.

DRAW CONCLUSIONS

1. What do you think caused the grapes to "lose weight"? How much weight did the grapes lose?

2. What substance in the grapes do you think the grapes lost as they dried up?

WHAT HAPPENED

The grapes "lost weight" when they lost some of the water that made them plump and juicy. The heat of the sun caused the water in the grapes to evaporate. During evaporation, heat caused the water to expand and leave the grapes through tiny holes in the skin of the fruit. The water then entered the air as a gas. Evaporation is a process in which water changes from a liquid to a gas. When you climb out of a swimming pool, the water on your skin evaporates into the air and cools you.

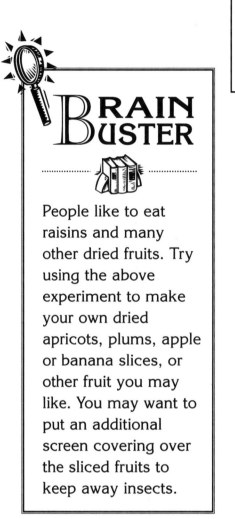

BRAIN BUSTER

People like to eat raisins and many other dried fruits. Try using the above experiment to make your own dried apricots, plums, apple or banana slices, or other fruit you may like. You may want to put an additional screen covering over the sliced fruits to keep away insects.

SAFETY FIRST

After you have weighed the raisins, make sure you wash them thoroughly in running water before you eat them.

Sail Away

Question: Can the force of magnetism work through a dish of water?

The wind makes sailboats move over the sea. Engines make speedboats zoom over the water. You know that the force in magnets—magnetism—attracts metals such as iron. Can magnetism extend through a dish of water so you can race boats you make yourself?

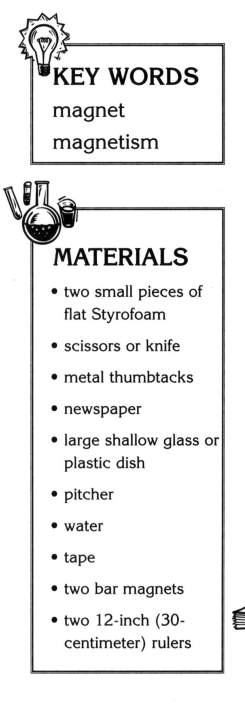

KEY WORDS

magnet

magnetism

MATERIALS

- two small pieces of flat Styrofoam
- scissors or knife
- metal thumbtacks
- newspaper
- large shallow glass or plastic dish
- pitcher
- water
- tape
- two bar magnets
- two 12-inch (30-centimeter) rulers

WHAT TO DO

1. Have an adult help you cut each small piece of flat Styrofoam into a boat shape with the scissors or knife. Carefully stick two thumbtacks firmly into the bottom of each "boat."

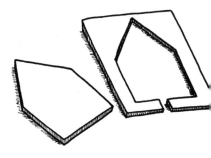

2. Make two stacks of newspapers. The stacks should be the same height, at least 3 inches (8 centimeters) high, and close enough to set the shallow dish on top of both.

3. Lay the dish across the stacks of newspaper. The center part of the dish should be exposed between the newspaper stacks. With a pitcher, pour water into the dish until it is about half full.

4. Tape one bar magnet to the end of each ruler. You and a friend each use one ruler to race your boats.

5. Place the boats (thumbtack side down) in the water at the starting line. Guide your boat across the dish to the finish line by moving the ruler and its magnet beneath the dish.

DRAW CONCLUSIONS

1. Can the force of magnetism pass through a dish of water? How do you know?

2. What part of the boats was attracted to the magnets?

WHAT HAPPENED

Magnetism is the force a magnet has on certain metal objects—for instance, on thumbtacks. Magnetism can pass through materials such as water. Thumbtacks are made from a metal that is attracted by the force of magnetism. That's why you could move your boat across the water. The magnet attracted the metal thumbtacks and "pulled" them (and the boat) in the direction you moved the ruler.

SAFETY FIRST

Have an adult use the scissors or knife.

Be careful not to stick yourself with the thumbtacks.

BRAIN BUSTER

Can magnetism pass through cardboard? Get some iron filings or have an adult cut up a steel wool pad for you. Lay a piece of cardboard on top of two equal stacks of newspaper. Sprinkle the filings or the steel wool pieces on the cardboard. Move the magnet around underneath the cardboard to move the filings. Sketch a picture or a design. Does magnetism pass through cardboard? How do you know?

Ironing Out Your Cereal

Question: How can the iron be removed from cereal?

Many breakfast cereals contain iron, a nutrient that you need to stay healthy. In this experiment, you will find out how iron—a metal that is attracted to magnets—can be removed from cereal.

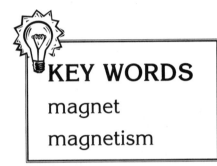

KEY WORDS
magnet
magnetism

MATERIALS

- packet of uncooked instant hot cereal (e.g., iron-reinforced oatmeal)
- plastic zip-top sandwich bag
- magnet
- hand-held lens (magnifying glass)

WHAT TO DO

1. Make sure the instant cereal you use has iron added (this should be stated on the front of the box or on the nutrition label). Open the packet and pour the cereal contents into a plastic zip-top sandwich bag.

2. Place the small magnet in the bag, too. Seal the bag and shake it well, for about 2 minutes.

3. Carefully, take the magnet out of the bag. Look at it closely with the hand-held lens. What do you see?

DRAW CONCLUSIONS

1. What did you see clinging to the magnet?

2. Why do you think the iron specks stuck to the magnet?

WHAT HAPPENED

A magnet contains a kind of force that affects some substances, particularly iron. Iron is a metal that is attracted to the force of a magnet. That is why the tiny specks of iron in the cereal stuck to the magnet. They were attracted to the magnet's force. A magnet's force is called magnetism.

SAFETY FIRST
Do not eat the iron specks separated from the cereal.

BRAIN BUSTER

A magnet will attract any object that contains iron. How many objects in your house contain iron? Test your magnet by holding it near various objects: hair clips, nails, screws, jar lids, and so on. If iron objects are small, they may move toward the magnet. If iron objects are too large, you may just feel a "pull" between the magnet and the object. What objects in your house contain iron?

For the Birds

Question: What kinds of seeds do different birds like to eat?

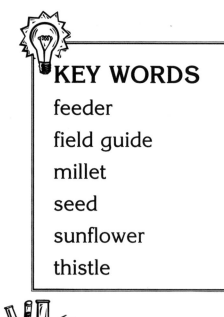

KEY WORDS

feeder

field guide

millet

seed

sunflower

thistle

MATERIALS

- five flat plastic dishes

- anchors for dishes (such as stones, clay, nails, or hooks)

- measuring cup

- birdseed (sunflower seeds, shelled unsalted peanuts, millet mix, cracked corn, thistle seeds)

- field guide to birds (available at a local library)

Have you seen birds around a bird feeder? Do all the birds like to eat the same kind of food? In this activity, you will find out.

WHAT TO DO

1. Place the flat dishes outside, about 4 to 5 inches (10 to 13 centimeters) apart. Make sure the plates are held in place well, using a stone, clay, nail, hook, or other anchor.

2. Measure 1 cup (237 milliliters) of each kind of birdseed you are using and place it on a plate. Make sure each plate has only one kind of seed.

3. From a window, watch the birds that come to each plate to eat. Notice the color of the birds' feathers. Notice the shape of the birds' beaks. In your science notebook, write or draw a description of each kind of bird.

56

4. Use the bird field guide to find the picture and name of each kind of bird that comes to your bird feeder. If necessary, have an adult help you. Write the bird's name in your science notebook, next to its description and drawing.

5. In your science notebook, write down
- how many of each kind of bird you see
- the kind of seed each type of bird likes to eat

DRAW CONCLUSIONS

1. What kinds of birds came to your bird feeders? How many of each kind came to eat? Did the same kinds of birds all eat the same seed?

2. What kinds of seeds did the different birds that you observed like to eat best?

WHAT HAPPENED

Different kinds of birds like to eat different kinds of seeds. Very often, large birds, such as blue jays with large, strong beaks, prefer to eat large seeds, like peanuts. Smaller birds, like sparrows, have smaller beaks and may prefer to eat smaller seeds, like sunflower seeds or thistle seeds. The size and shape of a bird's beak often gives you a hint about the kind of food that bird likes to eat.

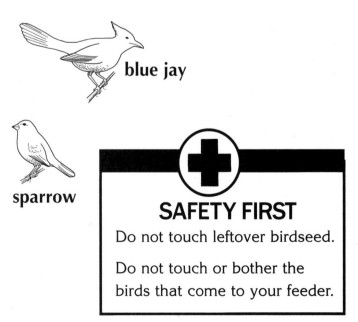

blue jay

sparrow

SAFETY FIRST

Do not touch leftover birdseed.

Do not touch or bother the birds that come to your feeder.

Looking for Light

Question: Are plants able to "look for" light, even when it's hard to find?

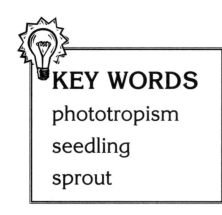
Why do trees and most other plants grow up toward the sky? You may have noticed that nearly all plants grow upward toward the source of light: the sun. Plants need sunlight to help them make their own food.

WHAT TO DO

1. Soak the bean seed in water at room temperature for 24 hours. Then, in the flowerpot filled with potting soil, plant the seed just under the soil. Water the soil thoroughly, but don't soak it. Keep the soil moist until the seed sprouts and the plant is about 2 inches (5 centimeters) tall.

2. Cut the two pieces of cardboard to fit inside the shoe box. Cut a window out of the left half of each cardboard piece.

3. Stand the shoe box upright, on end. Cut a large window in the center top end of the shoe box. Place the pot with the growing seedling at the bottom. Tape one piece of cardboard 2 inches (5 centimeters) above the seedling. Put the lid on, and place the shoe box in a

sunny window or directly under a full-spectrum light or plant-grow lamp. Watch how the plant stem grows. Don't forget to water your plant regularly.

4. When the plant has grown several inches (or centimeters), tape the second piece of cardboard a few inches above the first piece of cardboard. Make sure its window is opposite the window of the lower cardboard piece. Keep the plant in the light. Watch how the plant stem grows.

DRAW CONCLUSIONS

1. Did the pieces of cardboard inside the shoe box prevent the plant from growing? How did the plant stem grow past the cardboard pieces?

2. Did the plant stem grow straight or did it twist and turn? Why do you think that happened?

3. Did the plant stem grow out the large, top window in the shoe box? What do you think made the plant stem "find" the windows in the cardboard pieces and in the top of the shoe box?

WHAT HAPPENED

Plant stems grow toward light. This is called phototropism (foh-toh-TROH-pih-zum), which means "turning toward light." Plant stems turn toward any source of light. If light is coming through a small window cut in a piece of cardboard, a plant stem will turn toward that window. It will continue to grow through that window toward light. That is why your plant grew through the windows in the cardboard pieces and into the sunlight above the top of the shoe box.

BRAIN BUSTER

After soaking two bean seeds, plant each in a separate flowerpot. After they have sprouted, place the potted seeds on a sunny windowsill. Keep the soil moist so the plants grow well. Turn one flowerpot one-quarter turn every day. Do not turn the other flowerpot at all. Do you notice a difference in how each stem grows?

SAFETY FIRST
Be careful when using scissors.

Rooting Right

Question: Do plant roots always grow in the same direction?

You know that plant roots grow down into the earth. But how do they "know" how to do that? Will plant roots *always* grow down, even if a seed is planted sideways? In this experiment, you will find out.

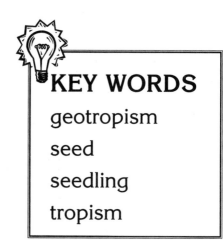

KEY WORDS

geotropism

seed

seedling

tropism

MATERIALS

- about eight fresh bean seeds

- bowl

- water

- paper towels

- two medium-sized wide-mouth clear glass jars

- plant sprayer (optional)

WHAT TO DO

1. Soak the beans overnight in a bowl with room-temperature water.

2. Stuff crumpled paper towels into each glass jar to fill each nearly to the top. Use the plant sprayer or flick water from your fingers to thoroughly soak the towels in each jar. Pour out any excess water.

3. Place four beans about 1 to 2 inches (2.5 to 5 centimeters) from the top of each jar, on different sides. You should be able to

see each bean between the paper towels and the glass. Each bean should be in a different position: pointed down, pointed up, on its side, on an angle.

4. Place the jars in a shady place, where you can watch them for several days. Each day, carefully feel the paper towels, which should be damp, not wet. If they're dry, use the plant sprayer or flick water from your fingers onto the paper towels until they are moist.

5. In a few days, the seeds will sprout. Roots will begin to grow from one part of the seed. Notice in what direction the seed's roots are growing. Do the roots grow in the same direction no matter what position the seed is in?

6. When the "baby" roots are 1 to 2 inches (2.5 to 5 centimeters) long, place one of the glass jars on its side. Watch both jars for several more days. Do the roots of the seedlings in each jar grow in the same direction?

DRAW CONCLUSIONS

1. Does the position of the seed have any effect on the direction its roots grow?

2. When you turned one jar on its side, in what direction did the roots grow?

3. What conclusion can you draw about how roots grow?

WHAT HAPPENED

Plant roots contain a chemical that makes them grow down toward the earth and the pull of gravity. The response of plant roots to gravity is called geotropism (from the word *tropism* meaning "turning toward" and the prefix *geo* meaning "earth"). Geotropism (JEE-oh-TROH-pih-zum) is very important for plants. Geotropism makes sure that plant roots grow into the soil to hold the plant securely in the earth.

BRAIN BUSTER

Do the roots of older, mature plants also show geotropism? Find a clear plastic flowerpot, or a clear plastic container, and a houseplant that will fit in it and still have room enough to grow. Make sure you can see the roots through the plastic. Place the potted plant on a windowsill, but *put the pot on its side.* (You may have to place something around the pot to keep it from rolling.) Observe the direction in which the roots grow.

Wear Plant Colors

Question: How can we get dyes from plants?

For thousands of years, people have used plants to dye clothing. Certain plant chemicals give plants their color. Some of these plant chemicals can be removed from plants and used to dye fabric such as cotton.

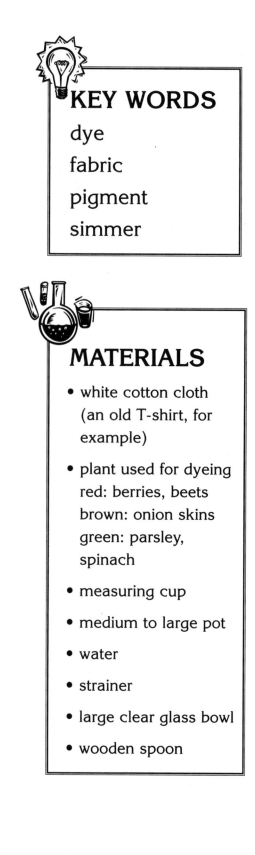

KEY WORDS

dye
fabric
pigment
simmer

MATERIALS

- white cotton cloth (an old T-shirt, for example)
- plant used for dyeing red: berries, beets brown: onion skins green: parsley, spinach
- measuring cup
- medium to large pot
- water
- strainer
- large clear glass bowl
- wooden spoon

WHAT TO DO

1. Decide what color you want to dye the cotton cloth. Get the necessary plant and chop or tear it up into small pieces. You should have about 1 cup (237 milliliters) plant material. Put all the pieces in the pot, and add water to just cover them.

2. Have an adult put the pot on the stove, boil the water, and simmer it for 15 to 20 minutes, stirring occasionally. When the water looks strongly colored, have an adult remove the pot from the heat and pour the "dye stew" through a strainer to strain the dye water into the glass bowl. Allow the water to cool.

3. When the water is room temperature, gently place the white cotton cloth in the bowl of dye water. Swirl the cloth in the bowl to make sure it is thoroughly wet with dye. Let the cloth remain in the bowl until it is the color you want it to be. You may "stir" the cloth from time to time with a wooden spoon. When the cloth is dyed, carefully remove it from the bowl. Squeeze out the extra dye water. Hang the cloth up to dry.

DRAW CONCLUSIONS

1. If you had wanted a deeper color dye, what might you have done to make the color stronger?

2. What do you think is the relationship between a plant's (or fruit's or flower's) color and the color dye it might give you?

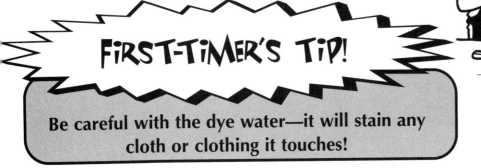

FIRST-TIMER'S TIP!

Be careful with the dye water—it will stain any cloth or clothing it touches!

WHAT HAPPENED

Plants contain chemicals called pigments, which help them use different kinds of light. Many plants contain lots of green pigment—that's why they appear green. The plants used in this activity contain pigments that are easily separated out of the plant. They are easily absorbed and held by cloth such as cotton. Cotton is a "fuzzy" kind of fabric. Cotton threads are made up of many, many tiny threads. Each tiny thread can absorb dye, so in this activity, the whole fabric became dyed.

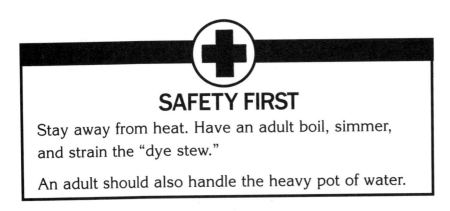

✚ SAFETY FIRST

Stay away from heat. Have an adult boil, simmer, and strain the "dye stew."

An adult should also handle the heavy pot of water.

BRAIN BUSTER

Do all fabrics absorb dye in the same way? Find another piece of white cotton and also a piece of white polyester fabric. Use the dye water you made. Soak each piece of cloth in the dye water for 15 minutes. Remove each piece of cloth and compare the two colors. Did the cotton and the polyester absorb the same amount of dye? Repeat this experiment to find out how well other fabrics, such as felt, burlap, or wool, absorb dye.

Under Pressure

Question: How can air pressure be measured?

KEY WORDS

barometer

humid

MATERIALS

- glass jar
- water
- light-colored food coloring
- straw
- centimeter ruler
- grease pencil or marker
- clay
- eyedropper
- tape

Sometimes you may notice that the air seems "heavy" and that it "feels like rain." You are right. Air may feel heavy when the air pressure changes. And sometimes, changes in air pressure do indicate a change in the weather. A barometer (buh-RAH-muh-tuhr) is a device that indicates air pressure. In this activity, you will make your own barometer so you can predict the weather.

WHAT TO DO

1. Fill the jar two-thirds full with water and add the food coloring.

2. Put the straw up against the ruler and, with the grease pencil, mark centimeters on the straw. Using small print, number each centimeter.

3. Close one end of the straw with a ball of clay, making sure it is airtight. Use the eyedropper to fill the straw two-thirds full with colored water.

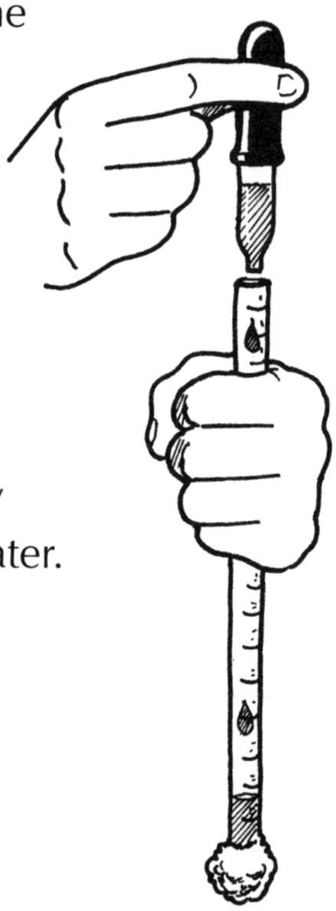

4. Cover the open end of the straw with one finger. Turn the straw upside down, with the clay end up. Tap the straw gently with your other hand until all the air in the straw is at the top of the straw.

5. With your finger still on the open end of the straw, carefully lower it into the jar of water. The bottom of the straw (with your finger on it) should be about 2.5 centimeters below the surface of the water. Once the straw is 2.5 centimeters under the water, remove your finger from the end. Tape the straw to the side of the jar.

6. The lower end of the straw must always be under about 2.5 centimeters of water. Because water evaporates, look at the water level every day and add water to the jar as needed. You may also add a bit of food coloring if necessary.

7. Keep a record of your barometric readings—the level of the water as indicated by the centimeter marks on the straw. Begin your record on a mild, sunny day.

Date	Time	Weather	Barometric Reading

Read the barometer at about the same time each day for a month.

DRAW CONCLUSIONS

1. What relationship, if any, did you notice between the weather outside and the readings you took on your barometer?

2. How might air pressure pushing down on the water have caused the change in the water level in your barometer?

3. How might you use your barometer to predict the weather?

WHAT HAPPENED

Air has weight. When air is "heavy," it may contain lots of water vapor. Then the weather feels humid, or damp. The barometric reading is low, indicating that rainy or stormy weather is ahead. When the air is not heavy and air pressure is low, the water level in the straw rises, and you know that fair weather is on the way.

BRAIN BUSTER

Low barometric readings indicate that a storm may be on the way. Sometimes thunderstorms bring dangerous lightning. Here's a way you can figure out how far away from you lightning is during a thunderstorm. Simply compare the speed of light with the speed of sound!

When you see a flash of lightning, begin counting off seconds (one thousand one, one thousand two, and so on). Stop counting as soon as you hear thunder. Every second you count indicates that the storm is one-fifth of a mile away. In other words, if you count 5 seconds between the flash of lightning and the roll of thunder, the lightning storm is 1 mile away from you. When thunder follows lightning immediately, take cover, because the storm is right around you.

You can calculate a storm's distance because of the different speeds at which light and sound travel. You can use these speed differences to locate a thunderstorm, since thunder is the sound produced by air heated by the lightning bolt you see.

Whipping Winds

Question: How can wind direction be determined?

Sometimes you can predict the weather if you know what direction the wind is blowing from. In this activity, you will make your own wind vane, which will tell you the wind's direction and help you make predictions about your weather.

KEY WORDS

vane

wind

MATERIALS

- small plastic container or pot
- pencil with eraser at the end
- grease pencil or marker
- scissors
- colored paper
- straw
- ruler
- long thumbtack
- compass
- clay

WHAT TO DO

1. Set the container bottom side up on a table. Have an adult use the pencil point to make a hole in the center of the bottom of the plastic container. Push the pencil into the hole, with the eraser end up.

2. Mark the four directions on the bottom of the container with the grease pencil or marker. You may indicate east with the letter *E*, west with *W*, north with *N*, south with *S*.

3. Use the scissors to cut out two equal-sized triangles from the colored paper. Then cut two short slits in each end of the straw. (The slits should be made in the same direction.) Put the base of one paper triangle firmly into two slits. Put the point of the second triangle firmly into the other slits. The triangles should be pointing in

the same direction. You have made a vane to move with the wind.

4. Use the ruler to find the exact center of the straw (not including the triangles). Mark the center, and at this point, carefully push the long tack all the way through the straw. The tip of the tack should come out the side of the straw. Press the tip of the tack into the pencil eraser. The tack should hold your vane securely, but the vane should be able to spin freely. Twirl it to test it out. If it's too tight, loosen the tack a little.

5. Put your wind vane outside. Use a compass to set your wind vane so that the directions on the container point correctly. After it is positioned, secure the container with a ring of clay around its base.

6. Record wind direction and a description of the weather every day or even several times a day for one month. *Note that wind direction is the direction from which the wind comes.* For example, in a wind that blows from east to west, the vane will be pointing east.

Date	Wind Direction	Weather

DRAW CONCLUSIONS

1. When you had the fairest weather, what direction did the wind generally blow from?

2. From what direction did the wind bring rain and storms?

3. Why did you have to use the compass to position your wind vane?

WHAT HAPPENED

Winds form when the sun heats the earth's atmosphere. Heated air expands and rises. Cooler air sinks beneath the rising warm air. As air is alternately warmed and cooled, the air moves. We call this air movement the wind. Sometimes air moves over an area in a predictable pattern. Huge currents of air may normally move in a certain direction. In some places, for example, people know that air currents moving in from the west bring rain. So, knowing the wind direction—in this case, westerly—can help predict rain. Find out about the course of your weather by keeping records of wind direction and weather for several months.

BRAIN BUSTER

See how heat causes wind. Turn an ordinary lightbulb into a wind generator! First remove the shade from an incandescent (regular) lightbulb. Let the bulb heat up for a minute or two. Then carefully sprinkle a tiny bit of talcum powder or baby powder an inch above the bulb. What happens? The powder "flies" up because the lightbulb's heat warmed the surrounding air, causing a current of air to rise all around the hot bulb. This current of air, which is like the wind, carried the powder up with it.

SAFETY FIRST

Be careful when using scissors.

Considering Clouds

Question: How does the form of a cloud help people predict weather?

You have probably noticed that there are different kinds of clouds. Some are thin and wispy; others are big and look a lot like cotton balls. Did you know that you can often predict the weather from clouds? In this activity, you will learn how clouds may tell you about the weather ahead.

KEY WORDS

cirrus clouds

cumulus clouds

stratus clouds

WHAT TO DO

1. In your science notebook, create a chart in which you can record the kinds of clouds you see and the accompanying weather.

Date	Time	Cloud Type	Weather

MATERIALS

• weather record (see "What to Do," step 1)

2. Look at the pictures on pages 72 and 73 of the different kinds of clouds. Learn what each kind of cloud indicates about the weather:

Cirrus clouds are thin and wispy, like white feathery streaks across the sky. Cirrus clouds are generally high in the air—usually about 20,000 feet (6,100 meters) above the earth's surface. Because they are so high, the water drops in cirrus clouds are frozen into tiny ice crystals. A "mackerel sky" has cirrus clouds that have become puffy, like tiny cotton balls. Cirrus clouds may sometimes create what looks like a halo around the moon or sun.

Cirrus clouds = fair weather
Thick cirrus clouds = chance of rain within 24 hours
Mackerel sky + lower, thicker clouds = rain within 24 hours
"Halo" around moon or sun = rain (or snow) within 24 hours

Stratus clouds occur nearer the ground in flat layers that often extend over large areas of sky. Fog is really stratus clouds that are very near the earth's surface.

Stratus clouds or fog = drizzle or rain
Thick stratus clouds = heavy, steady rainfall

Cumulus clouds resemble large tufts of cotton piled up in the sky. Often cumulus clouds occur in a clear blue sky. Sometimes, though, cumulus clouds may grow upward, swelling into dark gray storm clouds.

Low cumulus clouds in blue sky = fair weather
Upward-growing, dark cumulus clouds (thunderheads) = advancing thunderstorm

3. Keep your cloud record chart for several weeks. Check the sky for clouds as often as you can to see if clouds really do help you predict weather.

DRAW CONCLUSIONS

1. How accurately did cloud formation predict the weather that was ahead?

2. What other factors do you think affect the weather?

DID YOU KNOW?

Clouds are made of tiny droplets of water or ice. A cloud forms when water vapor or moisture in the air is condensed by cold temperatures above the surface of the earth. If a cloud forms very high above the earth where the temperature is very cold, the cloud will be made of water vapor that has condensed into ice crystals. If a cloud forms nearer the surface of the earth where the temperature is warmer, the water vapor will condense into water droplets.

Weather Wizard—Putting It All Together

Question: How can tomorrow's weather be accurately predicted today?

Use what you have learned to be a weather forecaster. See if you can predict the weather better than the weatherperson on TV or radio.

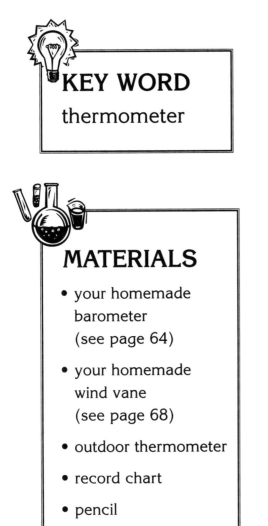

KEY WORD

thermometer

MATERIALS

- your homemade barometer (see page 64)
- your homemade wind vane (see page 68)
- outdoor thermometer
- record chart
- pencil

WHAT TO DO

1. Create your own outdoor Weather Center. After becoming an expert at using your barometer and wind vane, get an outdoor thermometer to tell you the temperature outside.

Attach it securely in a suitable spot outdoors, where you can read it easily. Try to keep it in the same area as your wind vane and your barometer.

2. Keep a daily record of your weather readings:

Date	Time	Temperature	Cloud Form	Barometer	Wind Direction

3. Use the following weather "clues" to help you predict tomorrow's weather:

FAIR WEATHER IS COMING IF . . .
- wind is coming from the west or north
- barometric pressure is going up
- clouds break up and blue sky appears
- the base of the clouds in the sky rises

FAIR WEATHER WILL CONTINUE IF . . .
- high barometric pressure continues
- temperature is steady and seasonal
- there is a clear sky at sunset
- fog disappears in the morning
- there is dew or frost in the morning

A STORM IS APPROACHING WHEN . . .
- wind is from the east and the barometric pressure is falling
- winds shift from south to north or west and the barometer falls
- the moon or sun has a "halo"
- the barometric pressure falls
- clouds get thicker, deeper, and darker
- low clouds move in quickly from the south or east
- the wind shifts to the south or east
- the temperature rises as humid air sweeps in from the south or east

THE WEATHER WILL BECOME COLDER IF . . .
- winds start to blow from the north or northwest
- the sun sets in a clear sky and a west wind dies down at night
- the northern sky looks greenish and clouds break up

THE WEATHER WILL BECOME WARMER WHEN . . .
- the night is cloudy
- wind direction changes from the northwest to the south

With this information, you should become a first-rate weather forecaster. But don't feel bad if sometimes your weather predictions aren't exactly right. Remember that predicting the weather is a tricky business—even for grown-up scientists.

Glossary

acid: any chemical substance that reacts with a base to form a kind of salt; a substance that turns litmus paper red.

adhere: to stick to or stay attached to a material, especially to a material unlike the original.

balance: a state in which things are of equal weight or value.

barometer: a weather instrument that measures air pressure.

base: any chemical substance that forms a salt when it reacts with an acid; a substance that turns litmus paper blue.

calcium: an element of many bases; an important part of dairy products such as milk.

capillary action: a force that acts on liquids to move them up and through tiny tubes, such as the tiny capillary tubes that carry blood to all parts of the body.

carbon dioxide: a gas compound, made up of carbon and oxygen atoms, in which flames cannot burn.

cell: the smallest structure that, when combined with other cells, makes up all living things.

chemical reaction: the forming of new substances when two or more chemicals combine.

cirrus clouds: wispy, light clouds high in the air that usually indicate fair weather.

cohere: to stick to or stay attached to identical material.

compound: any substance made up of two or more elements; for example, water is a compound made up of hydrogen and oxygen.

cork: the tough outer cells of the bark of the cork oak tree.

cumulus clouds: large, cottony clouds that may occur on fair days or, if they build into thunderheads, may indicate storms ahead.

dissolve: to blend completely with a liquid; to form a solution with a liquid.

dye: any substance that gives color, usually permanently, to a material; pigment.

erupt: to explode, as a volcano.

etch: to create a picture or other design by using acid to eat away an unprotected (unwaxed) surface of an object.

evaporation: the process by which fluid, or flowing, water becomes invisible water vapor in the air; a change of state from a liquid to a gas.

extinguish: to put out; to destroy.

fabric: a woven cloth made of materials such as cotton or wool.

feeder: a structure, designed to hold seed for birds, at which birds can easily perch and feed.

fiber: any material that can be made into cloth; for example, yarn.

field guide: a book containing pictures as well as written descriptions and information about plants and/or animals that people may see in nature.

fragrance: an aroma or scent; the smell of an object.

geotropism: the growth of plant roots in response to the pull of gravity; plant roots growing down into the soil toward the center of the earth where the pull of gravity is greatest.

grape: the fruit of the grapevine; a berry.

humid: when there is a certain amount of moisture in the air that usually makes people feel uncomfortable; damp or wet.

incandescent bulb: a bulb that burns with bright light and produces a lot of heat.

indicator: any substance that clearly indicates, or shows, a change.

inflate: to blow or puff up; to make larger.

insulation: any material that prevents or slows great changes in temperature; a material that prevents the loss of heat or cold.

invisible: not able to be seen.

lava: the liquid, melted rock that spews from an erupting volcano.

light-sensitive: refers to any material that changes or reacts to light; for example, photographic material.

limestone: a kind of rock containing substances that are a base, particularly calcium.

magnet: a piece of metal that is able to attract other metals such as iron.

magnetism: the force of attraction between two materials, particularly metals.

millet: a grain grown for food, similar to rice and barley.

molecule: the smallest unit of a substance, so small it can't be seen (it consists of only a few atoms).

oxidation: the joining of oxygen to chemicals in a substance.

oxygen: a chemical element that occurs as a gas (in the air) and combines with many other elements to form compounds (hydrogen and oxygen combine to form water).

phototropism: the growth of plants toward a source of light.

pigment: a chemical substance in a living thing that gives it color; for example, the green in green plants. Pigments may be used as dyes to color fabrics and other nonliving things.

primary colors: colors (red, yellow, and blue) that are part of the spectrum and can be combined to make most other colors.

prism: a solid crystal whose shape separates light into the spectrum colors.

rainbow: water drops in the air, usually after rain, that are struck by sunlight in such a way that they show the colors of the spectrum in an arc or circle.

refract: to bend, as light bends when it passes through different substances including water and air.

seed: the reproductive "package" produced by flowering plants.

seedling: a very young, growing plant.

silhouette: an outline; usually a dark shape against a light foreground.

simmer: to boil lightly, with a gentle roll.

solute: the substance that dissolves when added to a liquid.

solution: a blend of a solute and a solvent.

solvent: the substance, often a liquid such as water, that dissolves certain other substances (like salt) that are added to it.

spectrum: the full range of colors that make up "white" light; the colors in light separated according to their wavelength by a prism.

sprout: the tiny new growth produced by a seed.

stratus clouds: gray sheetlike clouds that usually layer solidly over the sky.

sunflower: a large bright yellow or orange flower that often produces hundreds of seeds.

thermometer: an instrument for determining temperature.

thistle: the tiny seeds of the prickly thistle plant.

tropism: the response of plants to stimulus in their environment. Phototropism is response to light, while geotropism is response to gravity.

vane: a weather instrument that indicates wind direction.

vibration: a rapid rhythmic movement; a quiver.

vinegar: a food item that is an acid; acetic acid.

vitamin C: a nutrient that is an acid; vitamin C is found in citrus fruits, tomatoes, and leafy vegetables. A body needs vitamin C to be healthy.

wavelength: the speed of a vibration, particularly sound; the distance between the tops of the curves of two waves: the shorter the distance, the shorter the wavelength.

wind: air movement caused when cooler air sinks beneath rising warm air. As air warms and cools, it moves, creating wind.

Index